TO CONTINUE

Poems by

Randy Blasing

Persea Books

New York

Some of these poems originally appeared in *The Denver Quarterly, The Literary Review, Modern Poetry Studies, Poetry Now, The Virginia Quarterly Review, Western Humanities Review,* and *West* (Smoke Press, 1980).

For information, address the publisher:
Persea Books
225 Lafayette St.
New York, N.Y. 10012

Library of Congress Cataloging in Publication Data
Blasing, Randy.
To Continue.

I. Title.
PS3552.L38T6 1983 811′.54 82-16513
ISBN 0-89255-071-6

Manufactured in the United States of America

To Continue

for Mutlu

CONTENTS

Asia Minor

TURKISH SPRING

plums suddenly
green enough to eat

a swarm of cherries
darkening the light

black mulberries
wind-bruised

tomatoes heaped up & glowing
in the sun like hot coals

apricots changed to gold
before your eyes

a rug
a garden of colors

the peach fuzz in the small of a girl's back
catching fire with the day

POSTCARD

The moon swells pale pale
yellow above the blue
red mountains. The air is so clear the eye
zooms in on the white city gone
a rosy pink across the bay, its lights
steady like planets. . .
For a moment, the light just *is*—
not coming from anywhere, marooned. Then
the sky deepens, the sea
turning black stops
at navy. Now the water starts to glow
in the dark like beaten silver
in the mushrooming night,
under the shadowy, lost stars.

IZMIR

The bright sky hammers in
the idea of blue. I step
off the ferry across a gap
of olive-drab
water, & in the square I see my first
urchin—there's a gun in his hand! It's black
plastic... Faces
fresh from work march
past me into the sun, a pomegranate
birthmark stands out
in the crowd. It figures:
the shoeshine boy
underfoot is shoeless... A pushcart full
of huge orange melons rolls
on by. I stop & read
the titles of the books
in stalls along the plywood wall
stuck up around
a construction site & plastered
with advertisements for this or that belly
dancer. Meanwhile a stack of new
sky-blue copies of *Capital*
arrives. To look
at the world the way someone blind must look
at dreams, to be sorry to die
because the world is turning for the better...

TOMORROW WILL BE NOTHING LIKE TODAY

A boy with striped
pajama bottoms ripped
in the seat for pants limps

down this back street
after his toothless young
mother. *Liberation*

is the word splashed
in red letters x'd out in blue
on the whitewashed wall up

ahead. Nearby a girl
all flowers ducks
into a door with two

black eggplants in each hand
like mortar shells.

BIRD ISLAND DAWN

Cypresses green as night
flare up here & there.

A flock of olive trees
takes to the hills.

Lines of high-waisted poplars
shiver, dancing in place.

A myriad birds
kibitz about the inevitable.

The sun is a blight on the night,
night with its honeycomb of stars.

MARMARIS

1. Castle Hotel

The royal-blue sea is spread out below.
Next door, the ruined castle from the days
of Suleiman the Magnificent sprouts
TV antennas tethered to the houses
standing in its shadow, built
with stones chiseled from it
over the centuries, whitewashed, & covered
with orange red-tile roofs. Beyond, green hills
of pines sneak up behind
the city strung along the shore, & islands
all mountains stonewall the horizon.
Purple-&-yellow swallows buzz
the balcony, while up above
the sky wears thin like faded denim.

2. Heat Dream

I am about to escape from the heat
by taking a plunge in the icy sea
when the three soldiers in combat
dress who pushed by us on the street
as we were walking out
to the beach from town reappear
marching back in
with a prisoner. His shaved head
is bowed & has a scar across
the top, with a fresh gash across the right
temple. Is he a deserter or one
of the visiting anarchists the cops
arrested yesterday? The steel cuffs
glint in the sun.

3. Morning

We climb down into town
for breakfast & get caught
in a funeral procession,
all men
trudging through the hushed street
in silence, taking turns
shouldering the coffin—a pine
box wider at one end & draped
with a green cloth, a vase of fresh flowers
at the head. The men all
look ragged as they do
in daily life, tattered
like a beaten army defeated even
before they started this morning.

4. The Quay

The sea is no longer
the blue mirror it was
on waking. All along the quay, the men
sit quietly smoking
in the rainbow of their colorful boats
as always, waiting to see what today
will bring. Will anyone ask, say, the *Orchid*
to ferry them to Paradise
Island clear on the other side
of the bay, the mountains smoky with distance?
But it's still early, the morning has only
begun! Sometimes you pray
for a life where nothing happens except
the ordinary: night followed by day.

BODRUM

At night stars like a fine rain
of light, then in the morning Cos
humping the old horizon through the mist
of distance & the sea

changing from slate to mica
to lapis veined with silver off
Black Island. On the beach
below, a woman in a pink

bikini spreads
a yellow towel under the green hotel
umbrella, & soon they all
turn out to bronze themselves.

This is our day! their colors cry
against the *shush, shush* of the water.

GLIMPSE

Coming back from the island on the launch
after swimming. A motorboat is going
the other way through the bright, dark-blue water
flecked with white. The shining
man in it has a face
full of lines from fighting
the sun. He waves, the kid steering us yells
something to him. He gestures back
as much as to say, "Can't complain,
I guess," & sails
by us, grinning... The day
won't end, or summer, it's a lie
we will die, we are made
of air, light, sea.

RAKI

Night of the long-faced moon.
The sea marble.
Through the moonlight

on the water, a boat ferries dark shapes
standing singing
across to the opposite shore,

the boatman hunched
in the back, one hand
on the tiller, leaning into the wind.

These are the shadows of the gods whose bodies
flamed in the sun today crossing the blue-
burning sea, shadows free now to visit

that other shore, drunk, ecstatic,
night of the Bearded Lady, yellow sleep...
All things are fire, all things water.

East Coast

LABOR DAY AT PEMAQUID POINT

Up to my neck
in blackberries,

I pick hand over fist
in the noon sun

until the sheen on them
goes to my head:

I think I'm blacking out
& seeing stars!

Hounded by thorns,
I stagger deeper

into the brambly
underbrush, hungering

for the blackest,
whitest fruit.

THE SEPTEMBRIST

The days fit you
with corrective lenses

Faces
in the street press
themselves on you
like the ruddiest apples on a branch

The blue sky is bluest
where the still-green trees are under fire

Their dark leaves jump
out at you like letters
in a headline spelling
the end

It's the same old story, but you're dying
to read all about it again

LUNCH HOUR

The plant drones on
behind me, still growing
out of the swamp it's slowly
sinking into, thus pressuring
the water table to give rise
to this makeshift pond of tarnished
silver goldfish
speckle copper, drawn
upward from snug
bottom toward the summery
fall day. A cricket comes alive
in a nearby stump, while some birds
maybe thinking it's spring
crank up in an abandoned stand
of rusted maples farther off.
The crazed
yellow jacket now hovering
around my sandwich woke up starved
after digging in for winter only
yesterday. Together we take
the breather time allows.

SMALL POTATOES

wind harvests the leaves machines the potatoes
gold flakes off the maple & showers down
on us we open our arms to the fall
& have the Indian to thank for this
summer that's doomed like his day in the sun

this morning I heard hunters popping off
off in the distance outside the window
the big old sycamore that used to drip
with yellow light I'd wake up early to
was gone machines made like birds in the back

a last monarch wind spirits it away blue
sky unfolds in the trees & the earth blinds

NOVEMBER SECOND

I walk around killing
time, early for my appointment

with the doctor. Trees dump
a windfall of gold dust

at my feet, the little whirlwinds
reap small

profit from the fallen
glitter. A young

kid howls
out nonsense, parents laughing in a downpour

of sun. To be walking around
on the earth is enough,

letting the gift
slip through my fingers.

SAILING INTO WINTER

A man stows loads
of yellow planks
in a cellar. Another
garages an outboard.

A chimney needs
shoring up, & gets it.
Roofers test their sea legs
in the sky.

Like the country,
I hunch
up my shoulders & knife
into the wind.

THE LANGUAGE OF THE FUTURE

Under the shadow now
of the loaded sky, words all end
in *-less: leafless, sunless, needless, speechless,*
penniless, homeless, careless, powerless.

By the same token, the other
side of the coin in currency is *massive,*
as in a tumor, heart attack, or air strike.

Every day a perpetual
state of emergency.

November 22, 1980:
a blood-orange moon surfaces in the steel blue
beyond the neon
shopping mall, balanced
on the knife-edge jet horizon.

SPREE

A passing car
catches the sun
skipping across

the rooftops & flashes
it back through the not yet
missing bare trees as if

from a nuclear
blast, freezing us
in the kitchen.

Outside, birds
(mostly house finches)
flit to & from

a feeder, sunflower
seeds everywhere.
We also eat & run

out into the cold
to go, today being
Saturday & the end

of the week, to go off
in search of food
ourselves,

our purpose
also nothing
more than to continue.

BLUR

white clouds
open on a blue sky

the sun blisters
the snowy fields with lakes

it's still early
February but the wind is

pure March
I'd know its big sloppy kisses

of air anywhere
I know this feeling

in my stomach
something between hunger

& excitement not quite
butterflies but more like

what happens when you see
green eyes

TURNING BLUE

for Mike & Karen Braziller

We scream at the wind & enter the world
of the park, which is full of life the last
Sunday in March. At first outbursts
of forsythia that isn't

witch hazel command all
our attention. Then a flurry of dogwoods:
"I forgot what they were." We all take stabs
at what some purple azaleas are.

A bunch of gray Chinese from the U.N.
flock around a woman snapping close-ups
of a jonquil. "They look like birds!"
in their everlasting tunics.

All of us locked in dreams of our famed strangeness
forget ourselves in the blessing of what is.

FOR TODAY

Daylight
bright as a dream. The trees, their green
still spotty, blur like the season
easing into focus. Birds take control
of the airwaves from treetops & high wires,
lording it over us
creatures here below. This morning
I feel like telling everyone I meet
to lay down their burdens
of the *Times* & the *Globe*...
All the cars parked up ahead on the street
mean church: forsythia blazing away
outside, the stony building there with big
closed doors, no windows, & no sound
coming from the people shut up inside
leaves me cold, like the long
shadow a funeral procession casts
over a day. I keep
on going to where bees preside
over crab apples snowed
under by blossoms, & I watch
as a Japanese-enough tree, reaching
the height of its glory
today, explodes
in a shower of pinks.

INDIAN POINT FOURTH

The dead wave their little flags from their yard
as we drive past
bruise-colored hydrangeas
to the beach. Picnickers in clumps
of two or three
wrap up in blankets, seeing clouds
muscle in on the sun. Far out
on the pewter water, sails flare
like candles on a birthday cake. We walk
the blacktop following the all-
rock shore, & a small plane brings us a message
from our local travel agent:
Escape. Rain scatters everyone,
no-see-'ems eating us alive.

West

WEST

for Mutlu

1. PROVIDENCE

We tear ourselves away from the Atlantic
at sunup & head on
out of the east into the blaze
of days, the lion of light breathing down our necks.

2. PURPLE HEART HIGHWAY

I see things through a silver haze
of heat.

The air is hot
as blood.

3. I-90 (MASS PIKE)

Blue hills bubble the horizon
as I go west
at last.

The quicksilver Connecticut
freezes in time.

4. I-90 (THRUWAY)

Late in the day we watch
the Hudson going to its death below.

The light stops & looks back over its shoulder,
leaving the earth.

The sky gets mauve
where the sun was.

The Mohawk stalks
the straggler day
into the dark.

Tonight the new moon starts
carving a place for itself in the sky.

5. DREAM LODGE

I crawl into the cave of sleep & take
refuge in dreams.

6. FINGER LAKES

"Take your boy to see the Mets yet?" a town
father at the counter of the Country
Bumpkin Diner asks the young guy sitting
next to him. But the guy answers
with silence, so he wonders: "Don't you have
a boy?" "I lost him five years ago;
got only girls now." My eyes fall
on the cutting edges
of the stainless-steel cream pitcher
in front of me. I look back up,
& the guy is long gone.

7. NIAGARA FALLS

Jade-green water
barreling over the Falls breaks
into a cascade of smashed headlight glass.

The poor souls getting on the boat
down below disappear
in black for their journey
into the mist...

8. I-75

The last summer my father saw, he taught
me how to stay alive on the road driving

this now-divided highway up
into Michigan on our way back home
to Minnesota. *Never drop*
below 85, he'd say, *watch*
the mirror for cops, & don't start passing
until you're sitting right
on the guy's tail. In the back seat,
my mother would turn white when he'd tell me
to gun it in the face
of an onrushing car, all 365
horses of the '63 Dodge
breaking loose at once.

9. US 2

Sun about gone, fish turn up dead
on the rocks of Lake Michigan.

Just after dawn I look into the woods:
night is hiding out in the trees.

10. US 8

I pop an Olympia on the shore
of Crescent Lake in Wisconsin & drink
to its lasting good health.

We drink in the *café-au-lait* St. Croix.

How could we have missed
the Mississippi?

11. MINNEAPOLIS

I walk into another death: my mother's
mother just shipwrecked here
94 years, 10 months, & 13 days
out of Bergen, Norway.

12. US 169

Down in the Valley of the Jolly Green
Giant, we pass the Minnesota River
& stumble on the town
of Henderson ("Pop. 760") where
my father grew up. It's a Saturday
morning, & along comes
the sheriff in his black
squad car to check
us out. He then proceeds to park himself
on the other side of the street to keep
an eye on our progress
down it. Instead, I cross him up by walking
over & asking him who knows
where my father lived. He
does, & points to a brick house I can't see
for the trees. He even
lets me in on my grandfather's strange passion
for eels... The name *Blasing* is still written
in stone on what was once
"our" drugstore but is now
the Legion Bar, a red-&-yellow sign
for Grain Belt Beer outside. The three kids hanging
around the corner turn
out to be Indians, the only life
in sight.

13. I-90

South Dakota, & the country
falls flat.

The gunsmoke-blue
Missouri: a surprise
oasis!

Across the river, sun scuffs green hills brown.

Rolling fields breaking up
into planes of yellow, green, & black drop
away on all
sides, extending our horizon
until we're circled by the sky.

This testing the limits
of space creates
a vacuum in my head...

14. MOTEL WEST

When we pull in,
a beat-up old white Impala is parked
out in front of the door
next to ours. Stuff is piled up to
& on top of
the roof of the car. It happens the guy
comes outside & sees we're not much
better off ourselves, so he asks us to start
drinking with him
& his lady. He left his wife
in Iowa, she her husband, & both
their jobs. Maybe they'll end
up in Reno & stay
with his aunt. He made the cooler
where he stashes his Pabst
himself. Over the roar
of a semi idling out on the side
of the road, he tells us how his good friend
O.D.'d at last after years of nightmares
about the war. Dusk falls
like a fine dust
settling. Strangers, we keep

on smiling as we talk,
the summer night rising around our ankles.
We wish us luck.

15. BADLANDS

In the Badlands we step into the future,
walking among the ruins of the earth.

16. BLACK HILLS

Rapid City shoots me twenty-five years
into the past to getting shaken out
of sleep & run out of town in the dark,
minutes ahead of a big flash flood.

17. US 85

This rainy Sunday
we shudder through lonesome
Wyoming toward sundown, so much nothing
burning a hole
in my empty stomach
like bad coffee.

18. CONTINENTAL DIVIDE

The stone-
faced Rockies cut
into the air & leave us all
gasping.

19. BOULDER

Today launches me on my thirty-fifth year
as I wake up
high outside of Denver, caught in the middle
of America, hung up between two oceans...

20. I-25

Blue mesas & low, sombrero-like green
mountains: it's suddenly
New Mexico, & I can breathe again.

21. US 64

Horse, I can see
standing in that yellow meadow,
nose buried in the book
of wildflowers!

22. TAOS

This afternoon
a mushroom cloud towers
over the Blood of Christ Mountains
back of Taos.

The sun sets orange-on-yellow, as on
the license plates of all the pickups here.

The gorge outside town dry-gulches
the meandering Rio Grande.

23. TAOS PUEBLO

Sky cruel. Always
scraping roof
of pueblo. No
ladder enough.
Doors & window
frames same bad
blue. Legs now,
too. The false sky
turquoise, & their eyes.

24. TAOS HIGHWAY

The sun just making it over the mountains
yellow-bricks the Santa Fe road.

We pass on
Los Alamos.

Tan Santa Fe wakes up
all rosy, an island of light
buoyed by air...

25. I-40

A smoke signal
of a cloud spirals out
of the hills past
Albuquerque, the code
unbroken still...

26. GALLUP

Big rigs looming out of the Sunkist west,
a massive lavender cloud trailing rain
off to the north, & the Santa Fe freight:
boxcars stampeding east into the night...

27. US 666

Window Rock, Sky
City: the Zunis lie
behind us, dead
south.

28. RUINS ROAD

Atomic Signs
Orbit Car Wash
Dizzy Land Liquors
Starlight Bowling

29. AZTEC

"The Pueblo Indian considers everything around him—the plants, rocks & animals, the sky, earth & clouds—his equal. All are alive & each has a personality. He is one of a highly formalized, ritualized group who, through prayers & chants, seeks to keep all things living together in harmony."

30. MESA VERDE

No lights below, & closer than ever to the stars
while still on earth.

Moon, you're so full of yourself you don't know
tomorrow the night will begin
chipping away at you.

Here in the presence of the Anasazi,
their cliffside condominiums
bring me the peace
of places where people have lived,
buried their dead, & disappeared.

We get to know
rabbitbrush, lupine, goldweed, Indian
paintbrush, scarlet bugler, & tansy aster.

Dumb hummingbird hovers
around my Coors.

Turquoise dreams
two nights running. . .

31. NAVAJO TRAIL

Sallow ground breaks
out in blotches
a sickly green.

Arizona
reddens.

Land so bad you
can't figure why
on earth anyone
would fence
it in is
nothing but
a reservation...

"You Are Now Leaving the Ute Indian Reservation.
We Hope You Have Enjoyed the Scenery."

32. GRAND CANYON

Sitting here at the edge
of the Canyon watching a blue
cloud block my view
of the sunset, I feel the pull of earth
two billion years away.

The sidewinding Colorado snakes down
through the ages
of rock in the distance.
Unmoving to the naked eye, it races
headlong toward its dream of the sea...

33. US 66

We descend into Nevada, rushing
west for the gold.

Blood oozes from the ground;
even rocks bleed.

& you, like love, guiding me down
the red roads, the main arteries

of this country,
seeking the heart...

34. LAS VEGAS

Vegas, the hope
of the hopeless.

All night
neon bushwhacks the stars.

An orange light
stops us cold where the sign
for Caesars Palace blocks
the *S* in "SHELL." Red letters spell
it out for us
this morning, & the day heats up.

35. I-15

The air thickens to a pink haze
above the Mojave,
as we barrel down the gun-gray freeway
toward L.A.

Suddenly the sky
is missing:
it's burned
to the ground.

We choke
on smoke...

36. THE BASIN

I plug the TV in & switch
it on, a face
swims up to the surface

without a sound...

We tune into the dream
& call it home
here as the sun breaks down
in the Pacific, another day junked.

California

FIRST MORNING IN CALIFORNIA

A jackhammer down the street
rips up the talk about
the weather. A hummingbird
slams on the brakes to feed on red
sugared water from kind
of an I.V. unit hanging
out from the patio, while a tiny
eagle frozen in flight watches from the top
of the flagpole. The sun looks like the moon
at first, then burns
away the haze. Some funny pines
bristle, & mountains brown
like old photographs. Soon
the street clouds up, the distance fails.

AT THE LOS ANGELES COUNTY MUSEUM

Face lifted to the sun,
a woman in white with blue sky for eyes
(mirrored glasses) leans back on a stone bench
outside the museum like that reclining

Aztec figure inside. The Aztecs worshiped
their mother earth in the shape of a turquoise-
eyed jaguar all mouth, the mother ever
ravenous for us, her children... The air

brings tears to my eyes, a breeze reminds me
of the black lake
of tar next door where plastic mastodons
fake going under, not the way

we open our eyes each morning to one
day less on earth.

TRUE COLORS

White fog hugs the ground
like beached clouds this morning,
& the day's paper announces it's

fall. Rain
comes down from the mountain
to the eucalyptuses' polite applause

at last, the sun-dried house
crackling like a fire...
Your shirt grows longsleeves

today, you make up lists of books
to take along wherever we
are headed now.

Outside the door,
the wind gives you the cold
shoulder. You smile to see a fly

slowed to a crawl. A moth the pink
you think flesh is
clings to the screen, its wings

laid out in all
their glory, & the yellow spider that
always flowered peach in the face

of the sunset has pulled
its net in & gone on
home to the dark.

PINEAPPLE

Porcupine
among fruits,

toy volcano
erupting in green flames

of leaves, plumed beast
at large in the house,

head of a housewife
tearing her hair out

in the kitchen, shrunken
head of some luckless islander.

POMEGRANATE

Thick-skinned apple
on the outside, inside
a hand grenade.

A dime
a dozen & to all
appearances bloodless,

but in reality
honeycombed with rubies
or bloody teeth,

seeds an army
might spring from, kernels
of Indian corn,

a hive of wakened bees
swarming inside your mouth,
blood on your hands.

IN THE OPEN

Sand
minus the sea. Pebbles swollen
to sheep-like rocks grazing
on mesquite. Quiet
like a stone dropping down a well
forever. I'm all
attention like a barrel
cactus, & as naked:
people mostly
blue like chips off the sky
appear disappearing
into the canyon, as ochre
boulders cascade
over the centuries. Last night,
half-dreaming before sleep,
I felt myself slipping
through the future into the past.
I was nowhere, but now,
losing myself
in the desert, here where everything moves
without moving, like the minute
hand of the clock I studied by the hour
in school, I enter the presence of things,
open & whole.

NIGHT MUSIC

Full moon spotlights the yard, two chairs
& a table empty
as they naturally are, you & I gone
as we must be...

I can feel the camellia bush stirring
itself in the shadows,
the innumerable tiny pink petals
spiraling out of the hard buds to be here
in the morning, surprising us
like the first stars
when we pull back the leaves
& discover them under there, blushing...

This is the moon
that lays us bare in bone-white light,
this is day seen
against the background of what waits ahead...

It's the blackbird in the lemon tree, not the tree
alone, yellow with lemons, that I love,
not mountains diamondbacked with snow alone
but blackening in the sun, rising out
of the earth like stored-up darkness,
not noon alone,
beast-sleepy, but the cat's eyes widening
at evening to take in the night.

VOICE

Out in the alley by the garbage cans,
in the light of half a moon glossed
over by clouds, & a few stars
including Jupiter
frozen overhead, an apricot tree

—an offshoot from the stump of a trunk
taken for dead & chopped down years ago—
rises defiantly
into branches ghostly
with blooms. Its skinny limbs shoot

straight up, like hands
raised in school—a whole class
of answers!—or rifles
finally reaching for the sky themselves,
surrendering to flowers after all...

Arrested by what I can only call
perfume, I pray for bees to come tomorrow
& set it humming like the plum
I saw—& heard—today. Tonight this tree
is news, not Jupiter & his circle

of mooning lovers flashed
across the screen. Listen, if anyone
in the future reads me, repeat after me:
Each March the same feeling—
just to be above ground!

ELEGY

Mockingbird, mockingbird,
never singing
a single note
once but always

repeating yourself, your song is
the music of monotony,
the sameness that makes all
the difference in the world.

SONORA WILDFLOWERS

All kinds pressed in a book no one can read
until the life is squeezed
out of them. Then
when you open to the pages
where they are, you find their million colors
gone, & flattened
they don't look anything like you remember,
your memory of them alive
erased by seeing them
this way—textbook lessons
in solid geometry, where the missing
dimension of depth gets left to the old
imagination, which never could fathom
busying one's head with fleshing out cones,
cylinders, & spheres. It's the same as when
the inevitable black camera shoots
to kill, freezing you as you were,
& the photograph takes
off on its own, wearing your smile
wherever it goes, no
souvenir of you but something that stands
in your stead, i.e., instead of the person
caught posing as you, you who are dropping
out of the picture at the speed of light,
the big picture, which you illuminate
with the flare of a match struck in the dark
the way stars do the night,
falling. Tomorrow already
filling with smoke & burning down
around you now, you'd panic if it weren't
for a walk in the shadow-swept spring desert
teaching you still is how to be.

LIVING IN THE GARDEN

Mornings all start the same
in the garden: oranges juiced
into a midnight-blue Guadalajara
glass you raise in welcome
to the sun (you who turned your back on *it*),
& then the light
sandblasting the slate of dreams clean (of even
the shitty one in which you wished you were
dreaming). The sky is everywhere
the off-blue of the shirt a man wears
keeping the grass down. Soon there are more
happenings in the smoke-filled air: another
tatterdemalion band of citizens
parades their cause through the streets to protest
their way of life, a truck
for Aurora Caskets
makes the earth itself quake
in passing. Eventually a huge
black-&-gold butterfly
comes weaving toward you, at which something
at the back of your mind whispers
snake. The nights smell of gasoline & jasmine.

MEMORIAL DAY

The jacarandas have blossomed
into a dream

come true: blue trees! The satiny
pink roses have gone

to pieces, ditto the black-
hearted scarlets. Downy fruit studs

the apricots, green thumbs
of hummingbirds

poke around in the last
of the bottle-brushes...

What does anyone
remember? Suddenly

the sky is grainy
with stars, our eyes crisscrossing

the abyss it is
any more: Orion's

Belt an ellipsis, the Big Dipper coming
up empty. We stand on the edge

of summer as on the verge of a promise
made to be broken.